D0991797

FOAL

North American
Animals

GROUNDHOGS

by Chadwick Gillenwater

Consulting Editor: Gail Saunders-Smith, PhD

Consultant: Kenneth B. Armitage, Professor Emeritus
Ecology and Evolutionary Biology Department
The University of Kansas

CAPSTONE PRESS
a capstone imprint

Pebble Plus is published by Capstone Press,
1710 Roe Crest Drive, North Mankato, Minnesota 56003.
www.capstonepub.com

Library of Congress Cataloging-in-Publication Data
Gillenwater, Chadwick.
　　Groundhogs / by Chadwick Gillenwater.
　　p. cm.—(Pebble plus. North American animals)
　　Includes bibliographical references and index.
　　Summary: "Simple text and full-color photographs provide a brief introduction
to groundhogs"—Provided by publisher.
　　ISBN 978-1-4296-8673-0 (library binding)
　　ISBN 978-1-62065-315-9 (ebook PDF)
　　1. Woodchuck—Juvenile literature. I. Title.
QL737.R68G55 2013
599.36'6—dc23　　　　　　　　　　　　　　　　2012002126

Editorial Credits

Katy Kudela and Megan Peterson, editors; Gene Bentdahl, designer; Svetlana Zhurkin, media researcher;
　　Kathy McColley, production specialist

Photo Credits

Alamy: Donald D. Lee, 21, Marvin Dembinsky Photo Associates, 17, SuperStock, 9; Corbis: All Canada Photos/
Stephen J. Krasemann, 19; Dreamstime: Roger De Montfort, 11; Getty Images: Alvin E. Staffan, 5, Paul Horsley, 15;
Shutterstock: David P. Lewis, 1, 7, Hway Kiong Lim, 13, John Czenke, cover

Note to Parents and Teachers

The North American Animals series supports national science standards related to life
science. This book describes and illustrates groundhogs. The images support early readers
in understanding the text. The repetition of words and phrases helps early readers learn new
words. This book also introduces early readers to subject-specific vocabulary words, which are
defined in the Glossary section. Early readers may need assistance to read some words and to
use the Table of Contents, Glossary, Read More, Internet Sites, and Index sections of the book.

Printed in the United States of America in North Mankato, Minnesota.
042012　　006682CGF12

Table of Contents

Living in North America

A furry rodent scratches its claws into the dirt. It's a groundhog digging a hole. Found in North America, groundhogs are also called woodchucks.

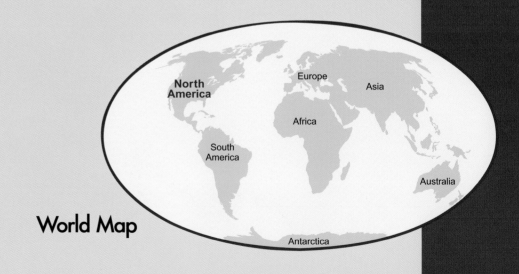

World Map

Groundhogs live near trees and in open fields. Their long holes, called burrows, grow to 45 feet (13.7 meters) long. They build nests of dried grass inside.

North America Map

where groundhogs live

Up Close!

Groundhogs have thick bodies. They weigh about 8 pounds (3.6 kilograms). From head to tail, they grow up to 27 inches (68.6 centimeters) long.

Like all rodents, groundhogs
have sharp front teeth.
These teeth never stop growing.
Chewing food helps to keep
these teeth filed down.

Finding Food

Groundhogs leave their burrows during the day to find food. They munch on grass, clover, and tree leaves. They eat alfalfa too.

In summer and fall, groundhogs
eat until they are very fat.
They hibernate from October
to March. Their fat keeps
them alive during the cold winter.

Growing Up

Groundhogs mate in spring.
About a month later, females
give birth to three to five pups.
Pups are born blind
and without fur.

Pups leave their mothers
after about two months.
Adult groundhogs live
on their own. In the wild,
groundhogs live up to six years.

Staying Safe

Foxes, coyotes, and eagles
hunt groundhogs. Groundhogs hide
from danger in their burrows.
They also climb trees
to stay safe.

Glossary

alfalfa—a type of grass

burrow—a tunnel or hole in the ground made or used by an animal

clover—small, leafy plants that grow low to the ground

coyote—an animal similar to a wolf

eagle—a large bird of prey that belongs to the hawk family

hibernate—to spend winter in a deep sleep; animals hibernate to survive low temperatures and lack of food

mate—to join together to produce young

pup—a young groundhog

rodent—a mammal with long front teeth used for gnawing; groundhogs, mice, and squirrels are rodents

Read More

Dunn, Mary R. *Capybaras.* South American Animals. North Mankato, Minn.: Capstone Press, 2013.

Kalman, Bobbie. *Rodent Rap.* My World. New York: Crabtree, 2010.

Phillips, Dee. *Groundhog's Burrow.* The Hole Truth! Underground Animal Life. New York: Bearport Pub., 2012.

Internet Sites

FactHound offers a safe, fun way to find Internet sites related to this book. All of the sites on FactHound have been researched by our staff.

Here's all you do:

Visit *www.facthound.com*

Type in this code: 9781429686730

Check out projects, games and lots more at
www.capstonekids.com

Index

Word Count: 211
Grade: 2
Early-Intervention Level: 17